Life
Reflected
In Verse

by

Gill D'Arcy

Best Wishes
Gill x
/06

Published by: Hilltop Publications

© Copyright 2005
Gill D'Arcy

The right of Gill D'Arcy to be identified as the author of this work has been asserted by her in accordance with the Copyright, Designs and Patents Act 1988.

All Rights Reserved
No reproduction, copy or transmission of this publication may be made without written permission.
No paragraph of this publication may be reproduced, copied or transmitted save with the written permission or in accordance with the provisions of the Copyright Act 1956 (as amended).

First published in 2005
Hilltop Publications
26 Springfield Road
Wincanton
Somerset BA9 9BL

Printed by:
ProPrint, Riverside Cottages, Old Great North Road
Stibbington, Cambs. PE8 6LR

Contents

Nature
Rain	9
Favourite Place	10
Walk With Nature	12
Our Garden	13
Snow	14
Winter Sky	15
Quiet Reflection	16
Emerald Lake	17

Love
My love	19
Love And Stourhead	20
When I Sit And Look At You	21
Silver Moon	22
It's You	23
I Love To . . .	24

Nostalgia
No 24	26
The Orchard	27
Sunday Memories	28
First Years At School	30
My Home Town	32

Family
Jessica	35
My Special Friend	36
Luke	37

Family Memories   38
Gift Of A Precious Rose   40

Sea
Twilight   42
Winter Sea   43
Empty Beaches   44
Sitting By The Empty Shore   45
Warm Winter Day   46

Reflection
My Teddy Friends   48
A Great Man   49
Trip To The Zoo   50
Teddy Bear Shop   52
Seasons   53
Bouquet   54
Raining Again   55

St Peter and St Paul, Wincanton

Foreword

Deep within the recesses of every human being there exist untapped resources of creativity. Some never find the key to unlocking them while others find them later in life. This book of poetry demonstrates the possibilities when such talents are released and the creative spirit allowed to flow freely.

Gill not only has a desire to put her verses into print but also wishes to allow this talent to be put to good effect. All the proceeds from the sale of this book of poems will go toward the restoration of her church of St Peter and St Paul, Wincanton.

I would commend this book as it weaves among the fabric of Gill's own life and the community in which she lives. In it you will find tongue in cheek humour, life encounter of joy and tragedy, local folklore and well known characters all portrayed with life and energy. As you read it enjoy the words and take a fresh look at life from the eyes of someone who has found the key to life's creativity.

Revd Stafford Low

Acknowledgement

I would like to thank my sister Beryl who introduced and encouraged me to write poetry.

To my family and friends I offer my thanks for their inspiration and encouragement to me, which has resulted in the publication of my first book.

My thanks are extended to Revd Stafford Low and Colin Winder for their contributions.

Lastly to my husband Richard who has endured the reading of them all.

Gill

Nature

Rain

Pitter patter on the pane
Outside it is pouring with rain
The sky is very dull and grey
I wish this rain would go away.

The garden that was dry and warm
Is now awash with this awful storm
Flowers are bending under the strain
How I wish it wouldn't rain.

Puddles forming all around
On the rock hard dry ground
It's bouncing high off the grass
I wish this rain would hurry and pass.

At last the sky looks much brighter
Clouds are parting to make it lighter
A watery sun is coming through
The rain has gone, the sky again is blue.

Favourite Place

Lunch is over we are on our way
We've both been waiting for today
Into the car off we go
Let's just get there don't be slow.

Into the car park here at last
Through the reception and turnstile past
Into the gardens what a delight
To me it will always be a wonderful sight.

Along the footpath we do take
Stop for a rest view to make
Talk about the scenery all around
My sister and I onward bound.

Ducks swimming on the lake
Children running bread to take
Down through Neptune's Grotto we go
Then back up the steep steps, oh so slow.

Past the little cottage on the right
In the winter the fire they light
Up to the Pantheon Temple for another rest
With such wonderful views we are blessed.

Next is the bridge where we have fun
Making lovely shadows in the sun
A little girl came walking by
To my sister she asked 'Are you trying to fly?'

We laughed and giggled all the way
Taking lots of photos to remember this day
Lovely scenes of the changing sky
Pictures for us to remember by.

Walk now finished back up the hill
Edible rewards to take our fill
Into the restaurant cakes and wine, really bad
Never mind it was a lovely day we had.

Walk With Nature

Along the footpath we walk
With each other we talk
The river is trickling by
Buzzards flying high up in the sky.

Hillsides are covered in purple heather
As onward we walk in summer weather
We pass by an old lead mine
Meadows and hillsides all entwine.

Sheep on the hillside are grazing
God's gift all around so amazing
Lush green meadows for all to see
As along we walk so merrily.

We stop for a well earned rest
With all of this we are blest
Nature is such a wonderful thing
Memories forever bring.

Our Garden

We are sitting here in the sunlight
A wondrous sight to behold
It's a small corner of tranquillity
Where colours are bright and bold.

There are many different colours
And several shades of green
Our garden is a wonderful place
All peaceful, quiet and serene.

It has taken many hours
To make this garden as it is today
The sun, rain and seasons all contribute
To ensure that colours will never fade.

So into a bright new future
All plants and flowers will grow
One day in our wonderful garden
Who will visit we do not know.

Snow

Silently from the sky it falls
Floating gently to the ground
Just enough to make snowballs
It came without a sound

It covers the earth in a blanket
So beautiful pure and white
Making such wonderful scenery
It happened overnight.

Roads and rail in chaos
When it falls so very deep
Gardens untouched by the beauty
Before shovelled in a heap.

Snow is the silent element
So quietly doth it fall
Causing such chaos and beauty
This winter time for all.

Winter Sky

Out on the pale horizon
Outline of trees are seen
The sky is ever changing
So many colours in-between.

The reds and oranges of sunset
As the sun bows out of the sky
Many rainbow colours
Showing for you and I.

As the evening draws in closer
And the sky changes once more
It's getting so much darker
Time to go home and close the door.

Winter sky is so fascinating
So many changes take place
Colours that are many fold
Reflecting upon one's face.

Quiet Reflection

In the stillness of the hour
Sat amongst the trees
Not a sound was uttered
Just the whisper of a breeze.

So many beautiful colours
Many of them a different green
A beautiful colourful reflection
Captured in the stream.

As quietly I sat there
Many thoughts running in my head
How wonderful is Mother Nature
At this wonderful garden in Stourhead.

Emerald Lake

As the coach slows down
Time to take a little break
Stopping here for all to see
By the frozen emerald lake.

Water's just beginning to appear
From the winter freeze
Trickling slowly at the side
Rippling in the breeze.

At the far side is a little house
We all walk in that direction
As we walk along the pathway
Looking at the new reflection.

Love

My Love

Your eyes are blue and sparkling
Your face so full of life
I was never more contented
Than the day I became your wife.

My love for you is endless
You're my husband and best friend
So many years we've been together
My hope is they will never end.

I love you oh so deeply
So dearly and so true
I can never ever imagine
My life without you.

So my darling this is written
To show how I really feel
My love for you flows deeply
And forever and ever it will.

Love And Stourhead

The lake looks really wonderful
The sky so clear and blue
We take this opportunity
To talk of love, just me and you.

We wander through the trees
They are every shade of green
The leaves are shimmering in the breeze
A wonderful picture to be seen.

Oblivious to all around
Just the two of us are here
The setting so romantic
Whatever time of the year.

When I Sit And Look At You

When I sit and look at you
Loving you the way I do
You're my husband, I'm your wife
I'll love you for the rest of my life
Together we are day and night
Being with you is only right.

I love you and you love me
That's how real love should be
I need to feel your body close to mine
Together we will always entwine
Loving you the way I do
When I sit and look at you.

Silver Moon

Casting shadows on the golden sand
A large bright silver moon above
Lovers walking along hand in hand
So happy and deeply in love.

The sea whispers on the shore
Making a gentle lapping sound
Who could ask for anything more
Than the paradise they have found.

Footprints in the sand there are
As they walk along by the sea
Thoughts of holidays way off far
Dreaming of things that will be.

Lovers walking along the beach
Enjoying their love so true
Everything is within their reach
Silver moon shining on a sea of deep blue.

It's You

The mornings are such a special time
Especially when I wake
To see you lying next to me
It makes my body quake.

Your face is still with sleep
When I look at you I see
Your rough unshaven face
It's just Heaven having you there beside me.

I watch you for a short while
Then slowly you being to stir
I love it when at last you wake
And your mind is still a blur.

Then I get my morning kiss
It's the best one of the day
You wrap me gently in your arms
Slowly all my cares fade away.

It's so warm and snug in our bed
No matter what the weather outside
It's you I love to wake up with
It's you I want by my side.

I Love To . . .

I love to look into your eyes
They are of the deepest blue
They sparkle like the stars at night
A truly wonderful part of you.

I love to kiss your warm soft lips
So tender soft and true
They are of the softest pink
I'm so lucky they belong to you.

I love to cuddle close to you
Beside a nice warm cosy fire
Enjoying the closeness we both feel
And that lovely feeling of desire.

I love to hold you close to me
Feel your body next to mine
You're my hubby, lover and best friend
Together we'll entwine.

Nostalgia

West Hill from Mill Street, Wincanton.

No 24

No 24 is a very big house
With kids, cats and maybe a mouse
This is the place where I was born
On a cold bleak November morn.

There were many rooms on three floors
With lots of windows and many doors
Scullery, living, best room and attic up top
No bath, four large bedrooms, where did it stop?

An attic where all the fun I had
It was filled with treasures some good, some bad
In this room I loved to come and play
With so much to do I'd visit each day.

The living room had a fire warm and bright
Where we'd sit and listen to the radio by night
By the window was grampy's sacred chair
Sit in it! Oh no we would never dare.

In the best room the piano stood
I'd go and play whenever I could
A very large window on cushions sat
I would hide and read and sit with the cat.

My home was such a wonderful place
I was lucky to have such a lot of space
I had lovely friends and memories fine
Of this lovely family home of mine.

The Orchard

Several assorted fruit trees
Scattered all around
Apples, pears, plums and cherries
Fall softly to the ground.

The goats were silently chewing
On the sweetest tasting grass
The geese were hissing noisily
As we all ran quickly past.

In the sties the pigs were feeding
Rabbits in their cages sleep
Mother weeding in the garden
An eye on her children to keep.

Inside the Old Mill House
The tools and toys are stored
If we were lucky we'd see a mouse
Happy days, we were never bored.

Our orchard is a child's dream
We used to stay all day
We never came back home clean
It's where we used to play.

Sunday Memories

On a lovely Sunday morning
As off to church I go
Hoping for some spiritual inspiration
Whether I'll get some I just don't know
Into the cool building
People all sitting in pews
Some are praying quietly
Others exchanging their weekly news.

The organ is playing quietly
I was remembering deep in thought
It was the same old church
At Sunday School I taught
Eventually as I grew older
Confirmation was next for me
I can still remember the occasion
In my new white outfit I can see.

I sang in the communion choir
Every Sunday morning at ten
With my friends all around me
In the evening I was back again
As the choir assembled each service
A tall lad who the cross did carry
I used to sit and gaze at him
Then one day in this church I did marry.

Now back to the present
As the service is about to start
It's the singing of the first hymn
That I can now take part
An hour or so later
Back out into the sun
Feeling all good and righteous
Morning worship now done.

First Years At School

Here we are at the gate
I really don't want to go
My very first day, mustn't be late
My feet inside go very slow.

I really don't need to learn
Playing with Mum is much more fun
When can I go home is my one concern
I'm missing all this sun.

Inside it really isn't so bad
My own new pencil and book
Maybe one day I'll really be glad
Of the time I bothered to look.

Slowly I adapted to my new life
Meeting my friends everyday
Reading, writing sums, oh what strife
Still we could always go out to play.

We did PE in a great big hall
Learning lots of new things
We threw bean bags, played with bat and ball
Skipping ropes made of string.

Pictures we painted, oh what a mess
Yellow, red, blue and green
Stories were told, I liked these best
Of giants, fairies and a queen.

As the years went by, I did survive
I found school was not so bad
Especially in the Hive, for class five
With our teacher the lovely Miss Ladd.

My Home Town

Sitting at the top of the hill
Looking thoughtfully down
Nestled in the valley
I see my hometown
Clouds are scurrying by
Sun is high up in the sky
I can see the church
Where we were married you and I.

Streets and roads all merge
Into the main High Street
Shops of many kinds
Cafes where we'd meet
Ducks swimming on the river
Children playing in the park
Games of football and cricket
Going home when it gets dark.

The very old part of this town
Where I was born and lived
Now I have a modern house
But loads of memories I relive
At the top of the street was a dairy
Daily deliveries all took place
At the bottom was a very old mill
Where often was a lack of space.

Somewhere there is the school
Where I went everyday
It was here I learnt
To make friends and to play
So sitting on this hill
I remember the town so well
It's been my home for many years now
Oh the tales that I could tell.

Family

Copywright G. Hiscock

Jessica

Ten tiny fingers
Ten tiny toes
Two lovely rosy cheeks
And a small snub nose.

With a mop of black hair
Two large brown eyes
Our baby granddaughter
Jessica arrives.

Such a heavenly gift
Sent to her family with love
Such a wonderful child
From our Lord up above.

At long last she's arrived
For her mum and her dad
Only they know of the past
Torment and tears they have had.

My Special Friend

Whenever I feel down
I only have to phone
I have a very special friend
Who'll help, I'm never alone.

We share so much I life
We laugh along the way
We talk about all sorts of things
She's only a phone call away.

We like to drink some wine
Also to eat naughty food
We do these things together
Especially, when in a mood.

We often talk for hours
About kids, music and books
Ideas we change a lot
And get some very strange looks.

We can laugh and we can cry
We know when each other feels low
Special friends are hard to find
This one I'm so proud to know.

Luke

On a cold November morn
Our little grandson Luke was born
His arrival seven weeks early
Hair all dark, wet and curly.

An incubator for him
Lights so very, very dim
Keeping him warm and snug
We all have to wait for that first hug.

Of his safe arrival we all were glad
Especially a proud mum and dad
Their family now complete
Just sister Jessica for him to meet.

Visitors came with cards and parcels
To see this latest arrival
Outfits, tiny teddies galore
Luke wouldn't want for anything more.

Family Memories

As I'm lying in your arms
So safe and warm and strong
My family comes to mind
It's together we all belong.

Many years we've been together
You're my husband, I'm your wife
We've had lots of tears and laughter
Throughout our married life.

We had a little daughter
Who brought us lots of fun
Then about two years later
Along came our little son.

Teaching them about life
Together as a family day by day
What fun it was to discover
Little things they'd do and say.

Now they have grown older
Each having their own new life
Both of them are now married
Living with partners as man and wife.

Our family has extended
With grandchildren, oh what joy
Our daughter has two of her own
Our son, a grown up boy.

Your love is always with me
My love for you so deep
Together as we grow old
Wonderful family memories to keep.

Gift Of A Precious Rose

Last evening I was given
This beautiful tender pink rose
It came from someone special
From her garden where it grows.

Petals of the most delicate shade
That matches this little girl's skin
Perfume so beautiful and leaves of olive green
Was given with such love from within.

The droplets of rain on the petals
Like the tears that were in my eyes
My granddaughter Jessica sent it
To nanny with love and a surprise.

Sea

Twilight

As they strolled along the seashore
Lovers walking hand in hand
They stopped to share a tender kiss
Then carved their initials in the sand.

It was in the twilight hour
Nobody else was to be seen
As along again they walked
Sharing hugs and kisses in between.

The sea was lapping around their feet
As they sat upon the beach
Quite oblivious to all around
Completely out of reach.

Lovers are often seen here
Walking hand in hand along the shore
Simply to be with each other
Who could ask for anything more.

Winter Sea

High are the waves that crash and thud
Beaches once sand now look like mud
Seas that once were calm and blue
Crashing and frightening for me and you.

Gone is the calmness of lapping tides
High and noisy in the sea rides
Pounding and grinding the shingle quite small
Fearful and frightening the waves rise and fall.

No more walking along on the beach
Everybody is kept well out of reach
At a distance we watch the waves form
A breathtaking sight at the height of the storm.

Empty Beaches

Once again the people are all gone
Beaches deserted no more do they throng
Sand is all washed new and clean
No more footprints where people have once been.

The sea still rumbles in to and fro
Up over the shingle where else could it go?
Splishing and splashing making of surf
Moving serenely here on this earth.

Winter is coming prepare for high tide
Everywhere preparing for another rough ride
It brings out the surfers who with pure delight
Ride through the waves such a wonderful sight.

Beaches now bare where once they were full
Dogs being walked giving owners a pull
Seashores deserted people now gone
Nobody left where the sun once shone.

Sitting By The Empty Shore

Sitting by the empty shore
Thinking about what life has in store
Watching the waves come and go
Wondering if the sun once more will show.

Thoughts into my head appear
Wondering why at this time of year
Everything shut and gone
Dullness now, where the sun once shone.

Footprints no more in the sand
Or lovers walking hand in hand
Watching the waves alone once more
Sitting by the empty shore.

Warm Winter Day

As we walked along the seafront
My love and I side by side
We watched the sea together
The gentle lapping of the incoming tide.

Waves all white and glistening
Sea a beautiful turquoise blue
Sun shining on the water
Just like my love for you.

Further along we wandered
Warm the sun up in the sky
Lots of people everywhere
Enjoying it like you and I.

As the sun started to go down
A chill came in the air
So we cuddled warmly together
Oblivious to all out there.

We love to walk by the sea
Watching its ever changing ways
Looking out across the horizon
On these wonderful warm winter days.

Reflection

My Teddy Friends

Furry friends I have so many
All colours shapes and sizes
They are scattered all around the house
My teddies in all disguises.

I have them in many rooms
Also sitting on the bed
My favourite one called Leo
Is a very big black ted.

They are all furry and fluffy
In several shades of brown
I love my bears so very much
Without my teddy friends I'd feel down.

A Great Man

As he lies in state for all to see
This great man of serenity
He was the one who gave us all hope
Now he's gone, John Paul the Pope.

Twenty-seven years ago he was elected
From many cardinals he was selected
None of us knew what a difference he would make
A great man of God as leader did take.

In the Vatican he made his home
Italy's wonderful city of Rome
Here he ruled over the Catholic world
This saintly man unruffled, unfurled.

Now lying there in his robes of ruby red
His trusty mitre placed upon his head
People in their thousands come to say goodbye
All with great sadness unashamed they cry.

Illness at the very end took its toll
He tried so hard to keep up his role
Then the Lord took his hand and said
'It's time to come home with me instead.'

He's now on his way back to his final home
One last journey before he leaves Rome
This great man who touched us all
Goodbye, God bless, Pope John Paul.

Trip To The Zoo

Up bright and early
We are off to the zoo
What will we see they ask?
Camels, elephants and zebras too
Two eager little children
Tickets we are to buy
Can't wait to get inside,
'Look nanny, look, look,' they cry.

We started at the reptiles,
lizards, snakes and such
Lying still and silent
They liked them very much
Off into the monkey house
Lots of swinging to and fro
Shouts and screams of delight,
How clever to not let go.

A peacock on the lawn
With feathers all spread wide
Then it's off to see the elephants
'Please can we go inside?'
They are so big and wrinkly
Their feet so large and flat
With trunks that are swaying
Into the mud they sat.

Next we saw the bison,
Onto the zebra cage
Passing by the camels
Who spit when in a rage
A baby giraffe with mum
Was the next for us to see
Feeding quietly in the stall
Guess it's was time for tea.

Finally a train ride
To see ducks, geese and flamingo
With great shouts of laughter
As onwards we go
Two tired little children,
A wonderful time they had
It's time to go home now
To have dinner with Mum and Dad.

Teddy Bear Shop

Teddies, teddies everywhere
On the ceiling, on the floor
Tumbling off the shelves
Almost falling out the door.

Many hundreds and thousands
Sitting waiting patiently
A brand new home
To be with you and me.

In their different colours
Red, blue, blonde and black
Some with bows around their neck
Others with humps upon their back.

It's a children's paradise
Children young and old
I love to visit my favourite shop
Many bears I get to hold.

In this lovely shop
Many happy hours I'll spend
Choosing which one is next
To come home and be my friend.

Seasons

Springtime brings the little lambs
Jumping around fresh green fields
Trees and plants start to re-emerge
Flowers all in their abundance yield.

Summer the days are hot and long
Trips to the beaches, bathe in the sea
With long light evenings for all to enjoy
Lazy days just there for you and me.

Autumn dressed in gold, red and bronze
From trees the leaves are all falling
Animals into their hibernation go
Ready for the winter now calling.

Winter known as a cold time of year
We are all snuggled around the fireside
Children all wrapped warmly in scarves and hats
Through frosty windows we peek outside.

Seasons they come and seasons they go
New life and changes they are bringing
How lucky we are to see them all
Nature is always re-arranging.

Bouquet

Stocks standing tall and slender
Roses so delicate and pink
Carnations with feathery petals
They will need water to drink.

Lilies tender pink and white
Gerber's off the palest cream
Chrysanths with heads a plenty
A bouquet fit for a queen.

Raining Again

Raining again, another dark, dismal day
Wishing this rain would just go away
Summer seems so far long gone
Those lovely long days when the sun just shone.

I'll sit by the window watching the droplets run
Wishing for a little glimpse of the sun
Puddles are forming everywhere I look
Guess I'll just read another page of my book.

To all humans...the tools you need to remind yourself that YOU'RE ok.

Acknowledgments

Thankyou Donna Chatzikos for being my spiritual guide. Natalie Wheeler, for being my mentor, friend and for believing in me. Naomi Matzen for proof reading my work and keeping cheering me on. I will be forever grateful.

Contents
Opening
Digital detox
Body
Weight loss Journey – The Gym
FOOD - I love you I love you not
My Spiritual Journey
Stars and Umbrellas
Values
Meditation
The Green-Eyed Monster
Mother Nature – a Woman's thoughts
Wake up and Makeup
Am I Normal?
MEDITATION

Opening

Hey, you, my name is Vikki. On the 14th of December 1988, I made my way into this very large world, a place we call earth, where humans are born every minute. Every unique human is then raised into society, whether it be by their family, support groups, foster parents or another human that may take them under their wings. Humans do not choose where or by whom they are raised, but as they evolve, choices can be made, and paths can be determined according to that humans' interests and goals. Choice is life's golden ticket.

You might be wondering who I am and why I think my advice, or my experiences mean anything to you. I'm a regular woman from Milton Keynes. Every celebrity, social influencer, NBA player and the next Love island cast have made choices and will continue to make them for the rest of their lives. Every single human makes choices, makes mistakes, learns lessons, has a period (women), pay bills, does the laundry, communicates, eats and the list goes on and on. So regardless of the money you earn or the social status you have, you will be making choices and have your own unique mind and body just like me.

I am human. So, therefore, sharing my stories and my tips to overcoming obstacles in life that may spark the question, 'am I normal?' may help, comfort or even reassure you that we are all human and you are not alone.

I don't remember being a child. There's a lot I can't remember; my first day of school, learning to ride a bike or playing with my friends. I know how I felt if someone or something reminds me, but I can't seem to access the memories. This doesn't mean I had a bad childhood. Some people remember everything from their childhood. Does that mean I'm not normal? Of course, I am. We all learn and process life in a different way. Some people have clear memories and recall everything by word or date. Others learn and remember by feeling and that's ok.

The reason I mention my memory is that most psychologists or therapists will tap into your past to understand why you act or react in a certain way. However, because I find it hard to remember my past I believe that overcoming obstacles in life is a case of living in the now and looking forward to better days.

With that said, I will unravel some of my life in this mini comfort book. Life involves thousands of choices that will impact your future. Life is a set of lessons, blessings, and choices. Now at the ripe age of 30, battling with weight loss, stuck in the 'which career do I want' choice, saving for a mortgage and on a journey of self-discovery, I am evolving every day into the woman I want to be.

The BIG question I have had over the last 10 years is 'Am I normal?'. I bet you have asked yourself that at least once. Have you been stuck in big life choices, or wondered whether the way you think is the same as someone else? If so, continue reading. You may learn a little something, feel relieved or simply feel at peace with some of your choices.

I believe that all humans are placed on this earth for a reason. Everybody has a purpose, and once in touch with that idea, they can create and become the best version of themselves.

I decided to write this book because I believe that my purpose is to either educate or inspire others in their journey through life. Tired of thinking what I can do in life, trying to plan every step, worrying about money and fearing the unknown, I decided I would live in the moment and do what I love rather than doing what I am able to do. Anyone can do pretty much anything If they put their all into it, but what's the point, if you don't enjoy it?

Some people are money focussed, other family focussed. Some are happy to work just to pay the bills and get through life, while others have big dreams and master plans which will bring them money, everything they want and make a difference in the world. I say if it makes you happy then do it. If it doesn't, then change it.

I was very confused and didn't know what I wanted, but there are so many factors in my life that affected my needs and desire. As I begin to take you through my experiences, you will understand and hopefully be inspired by my journey. Only up until now, did I realise what effect my choices had on my life. I do not regret anything in my past, because that's what made me, me. However, I did learn from my mistakes and I am hoping that once you have read this book, you can take away some useful and motivating lessons that you can apply to your life. Life is about learning because, at the end of the day, Knowledge is power.

Each section of this book is part of my umbrella of the body. Why Umbrella I hear you say? Well, in one of my mentor sessions, my mentor explains journeys in life to me as Stars and Umbrellas. Me being the star and my journey as the Umbrella. Each spike of the Umbrella is a different step of that journey, and once all spikes are up, the umbrella is erect, and the journey is complete.

Sometimes, the wind pulls you this way and that way and the umbrella may turn inside out, but that's ok, you can always fix it, and if you can't fix it, get a new one. I had been thinking about writing this book for a couple of years before I had this meeting with my mentor, and suddenly it clicked. What a great way to interpret a journey.

You may have hundreds of umbrellas, small ones, big ones, broken ones, and new ones. For me, I knew I wanted to inspire, help and capture my readers through my own experiences. I am writing this book from the heart and I hope you can take something from it.

Wait, one last thing before you continue! Whether you are young, old, rich or poor, lonely, in love, having a midlife crisis or simply so happy with everything in your life it couldn't get better…. please read this book with an open mind. By that I mean try not to compare your life with mine, or someone else's life. If anything at all, I want you to be comforted by this book, understand that everyone is different and that we are all human, we are made to love and to accept each other.

If you can relate to some of the stories in this book, I hope it inspires you and gives you that realisation that you are not alone. We all struggle sometimes, we all need a bit of encouragement, but mostly, is that when we die, no one will remember us for the car we drove, how many abs we had, the house we lived in, what phone we had or how expensive our bag is. People will remember you for the support you gave, being a friend, loving your family and bringing people together. People will remember you for you, remember that.

So, this is the first book of the comfort series about my journey through weight loss and acceptance of my body. A few friends have told me that I should do this, and I thought 'oh why not let's give it a shot'. Although primarily I'm going to share with you my experience of weight loss and fitness, you will notice I draw on other topics that have affected my journeys, such as heartbreak, depression and loss. If you like this little book of comfort, then you will find Am I normal? #02 Mind helpful too.

DETOX

2

#Digitaldetox

Before I begin, the first tool I can give you is a DIGITAL DETOX. Over the years, social media and the news have played a huge role in the choices that people make. For me, I didn't realise how much of an effect it was having on my day to day life. Battling body issues and mental problems, spending half of my day scrolling through Instagram and Facebook was distorting my view of the world. After a huge argument with my boyfriend and then checking on social media whether he had dumped me (I know, how sad), I realised that my mind was out of control and my life was being written by the actions of a digital world.

To some people, social media is like a drug. Addicted to the 'like' and the 'comment' and the 'follow', to some people it's inspiring and a way of keeping up to date in the world: It can be positive and negative. For me, it was becoming a time filler and an addiction to comparing myself to others. I would deny this, and even lie to myself and say that it was inspiration and motivation for me. But endless photos of half-naked woman and relationship statuses are just not something I am willing to determine my life by.

So, for over a month I deactivated all my accounts and deleted the apps from my phone. At first, it was like I was on autopilot and I kept going to check my notifications, but they weren't there. It felt a little odd, wondering what to fill my time with. But after a few days, I realised I was living in the real world. Speaking to more people, seeing and noticing things I never really noticed before. It almost felt like I was being reborn. I was finally able to finish this book because I was using my time better and focussing on the things that meant something to me.

If you take anything from this little book of comfort, I urge you to try a digital detox. It can be a day, a week, a month or even a year. I promise you, you will gain more than you expected. Some of these potential benefits are listed below:

- ❖ Lift your mood
- ❖ Live in the moment
- ❖ Stop obsessing over the past
- ❖ Gain Free time
- ❖ Reconnect with the outside world
- ❖ Stop competing with others
- ❖ Sleep better

3

Body

Do you look in the mirror and cringe?

Do you see a picture of yourself and feel disgusted?

Do you not see what others see when they look at you?

Are you normal? Yes

Every single person whether male or female has or has had some type of insecurity about the way they look. The media enforces a standard of how we should look, and these are unrealistic standards. We all have one body that we were born into, different shapes, sizes, height, build, blood type, skin type, etc. Working on your health and wellbeing is one of the most effective ways to love yourself and show gratitude to your own body.

Whether you're a size 6 or 22, who has the right to judge you? The world has grown into a place of judgment, comparisons and jealousy. Now that's unhealthy.

I'm on my journey to love myself, and albeit a cliché, if you love yourself then you will be loved. For the last 10 plus years, I have had body confidence battles. Losing weight, gaining weight, eating disorders, loss of self-worth and the list goes on.

Typically, all women and men struggle at some point in their lives with their image and it's no doubt because of the pressure society puts on us through social media and celebrity lives.

With many editing apps such a photoshop we can create an image of how we want others to see us. There's nothing wrong with a filter but models today are being photoshopped to the extreme. This gives the world a false sense of perfection.

What we forget so easily is that our bodies are our HOUSE. A home for everything that makes us work as humans. If we don't look after this house, then how can we expect to live happy healthy lives?

My weight loss journey began many years ago. I have always struggled with my body weight, self-confidence, and food-related issues. But, just over 3 years ago I began to view my weight loss issues and my fitness goals from a different perspective. An old friend once said to me 'you are unique, this is your life Vikki, set your goals and smash them'. So, on 1st January 2016, I decided I had to do something for myself and the one thing I had always wanted was to be happy in my body, because let's face it, we only get one to live in.

The same friend also introduced me to 'The Secret' and the law of attraction about 2 years ago. I won't go into it now, but it has changed my way of thinking completely.

http://www.thesecret.tv/

Check this website out if you're intrigued. The power of positive thinking is insane.

My mindset before my journey began was 'I can't', 'but I've failed before', 'what's going to be different this time?', 'I like food too much' etc. But something this time did change. I had a new support system and I had been broken down too many times that I found comfort in doing something just for myself.

Since joining the gym, I have made a ton of friends who support me, show me new workouts, encourage and understand me. Sometimes, going out of your comfort zone and just listening is one of the best things you can do. KNOWLEDGE IS POWER. I believe that. But it's how you use that knowledge that is important.

Now don't get me wrong, this is probably one of the hardest 3 years of my life so far. Overcoming anxiety in the gym, not binging on everything I can get my hands on, changing jobs twice, having relationship and personal issues arise and generally dealing with life has been so tough. But that switch in my mindset has saved me, and every time I get a knock, I bounce back now like an Olympic trampolinist.

So far on my journey, I have lost 4 stone, dropped 2 dress sizes and gained a whole load of confidence. Now, you might be wondering why I've only dropped 2 dress sizes? Well the thing is, I began to like my shape and I didn't want to lose it. So, I focussed on weight training and building muscle in the areas that my fat was coming off. Weight training has made me stronger, more toned and kept my womanly curves. My goal this year is to lose a few more stones and build a beautiful house to live in.

If anything, the best feeling is seeing change. It's my motivation. The thing with weight loss is that all the pressure from magazines, social media and reality TV shows give an 'ideal' body. But do what makes you happy. There's no such thing as an ideal body or a normal body. If you're healthy and comfortable in your skin, then that's all that matters.

DIET DIET DIET which DIET works?

The Truth is' DIET' isn't a long-term solution or positive word. A healthy lifestyle is my way of looking at it. Calories in calories out is the most trusted way to lose weight.

Diets are everywhere. On social media, YouTube, TV and more. Everywhere you look there is a new 'guaranteed weight loss system'. But, after years of yoyo dieting and many will agree, Dieting is a short-term fix. The one trusted way to drop those pounds is a healthy balanced diet and more exercise.

The 'BMI' scale is also a little bit untrustworthy because a 5'5 shapely woman with muscles too is not going to weight 9 and half stone just to say she is healthy. A 5'5 woman with hips, muscles, a good blood pressure, good fitness levels and glowing skin is going to say she is healthy.

The way I see it is, if you feel fit and healthy and your house is glowing, then you are healthy.

Happiness is the goal and if you feel happy inside and out then you have succeeded. If you're not quite there yet whether you hold too much weight or even too little weight and you're feeling sluggish and tired, then don't worry because it's something you can change.

One of my biggest lessons whilst on my journey has been discovering the art of change. If you can't change it, then don't worry about it. If you can change it then get your umbrella and begin your journey.

SWEAT

4

Weight loss Journey – The Gym

OMG everyone is looking at me!

What if i can't do the exercise?

What if my bum sweat is on the seat?

Why are they looking at me?

If you haven't said something like this when you walk in the gym, then you're a confident gym bunny and if you have then maybe you have a little bit of social anxiety in the gym?

All i know is i had bad anxiety when i started going to the gym. When i say bad i mean, I'd drive to the gym then I'd drive straight home, or I'd go in the gym and then go and hide and cry, i even once pretended i felt sick and just got my stuff and left. Next thing you know I'm in bed watching Pretty little liars with a share bag of Maltesers.

I've never been small and always loved food, but a few years of my life from 21-27 I had some very unpleasant relationships, a hard time finding myself and ultimately just struggling with life. I turned to food as a comfort (as many of us do) and over time just piled on the pounds without even realising. So, I decided to change my life, but I had no idea what I was doing.

ANXIETY STRUCK!

My weight always held me back. Socially, at work and in relationships. The experience in relationships had broken me down and i ended up losing all my self-worth, confidence and purpose. My friends and family were always my biggest support, but when you're that far down, nothing can bring you up because you don't know why you're there.

Am I normal? Yes

I suffered from bad skin conditions, lost my job and became ill because of the stress and anxiety ultimately made everything a lot worse. It was a vicious cycle. stress...illness...food...weight gain...stress...illness...food... weight gain. Being bigger held me back because i had no confidence in myself which is the worst place to be.

However, i don't regret or get upset because of the past, it has made me a stronger person today. Whatever path you're on, whoever is in your life right now and whatever happens next, it can always be changed because as humans, we are very lucky to be able to manipulate our lives and make it the way we want it to be.

What made me anxious in the first place you're probably thinking?

A BOY. The funny thing is, I had one comment when I was 10 years old where a boy at school said I had 'double knees' and I have never worn shorts or a dress above my knees for that reason. However, I've never had any nasty comments even when I was at my biggest, in fact, the complete opposite.

Sometimes you don't see what others see in you and that's always been my issue. After losing 4 stone, I had a comment when I was out, and someone called me fat which did for a moment kick my confidence. After losing all that weight and for only now someone to comment on my appearance, I was confused. I also plucked up the courage to wear a shorter dress that evening, but I didn't feel comfortable and to get a comment like that was the icing on the cake. For me, that comment about me stuck in my subconscious and as I grew up, relationships with boys were not too pleasant for me. Toxic relationships that made me feel selfless and worth nothing was a normal thing for me. Jealous men who didn't want me to have fun or have any friends, they just kept coming along.

I then realised that the only way I would ever be happy was to start loving myself and using every day to make myself a better person. After the last episode of controlling and manipulative behaviour I decided enough was enough for me. Either I stay single or wait until someone comes into my life who will support me, grow with me and bring out the best in me.

Without my friends and family, I would never have built up the confidence I have right now. Support is so important.

Tool: always reach out and talk. Whether its friends, family or an anonymous email service, letting out your feelings will help.

I met someone a few years ago who introduced me to the law of attraction, it's the one belief I fall back to every time that keeps me positive. Please read about the law of attraction if you haven't yet. I will never forget what my friend said to me, 'if you can see it and believe it, then you can achieve it'. From that day forward and after completing the book, I now know why everything happens in my life. If it's rubbish, I know why, if it's good, I know why, it's all about controlling your thoughts. You can make the rest of your life the best of your life.

What made me change my life?

After I completed my makeup artistry course in London, i looked at some pictures and realised I was so unhappy every time I looked in the mirror. When I was sitting in front of the mirror doing practical work for my course, I found it hard to look at myself without cringing. Travelling to London every day, sweating on the tube and feeling so uncomfortable just got the best of me. I'd look at Instagram and other social media and be inspired by fitness models and really wanted to believe I could be like that.

In December 2015 I met a friend and she encouraged me to go to the gym with her as she was on the same journey. I wanted to be something that people thought I'd never be, but mainly I wanted to prove to myself that this was it, and this opportunity was too good.

Funny enough one of best mates Danielle, said to me a couple of months in, 'this time you're going to do it, I've got a feeling' and she was right. She was there for me through all the bad times and this time she knew I was serious and something in my mind had changed. A few years later she is still saying ' I knew you would do it' and supporting me constantly. I'm lucky that I have friends who have supported me the whole way through.

My friends have helped me get through my anxieties in the gym but also helped me believe in myself.

The gym I joined was big and had a woman's only section. I started off in that area because there was a max of 5 people in there every time I went. This helped me get used to walking into the gym and using the machines. Walking into the gym was probably the hardest thing for me back then, because it was like another world. I had one training session with a PT and that helped me with understanding what my body could do and where I wanted to go with this journey.

FITIBT! A game changer

For my 30th Birthday I asked for a Fitbit, so I could keep an eye on my activity level. What a great way to track your movement, sleep, calories and more. For the women out there, you can even track your Aunt flo. The Fitbit app allows you to compete with friends and family to see who can do the most steps. It's so motivating.

The average goal is 10,000 steps a day, but I set mine to 12,000 so I could push myself and make sure I move more. If you find yourself going to work, sitting at a desk all day then going home to sit on the sofa, I highly recommend getting a Fitbit or any other wearable tracker. Even if you're not hitting your daily target it reminds you to just get up and move a little more. Baby steps are key to longer term benefits.

My goals now

I still have a few stones to drop in weight, however, I want to keep my shape and have been weight training since day one which has been perfect for me because I now love my shape.

I'd love to inspire and show women that anyone can do it. I want to keep my womanly curves and I want to show the world that anyone can do this. I feel so much happier in myself now and things can only get better from here. Don't get me wrong, I have days or even weeks where my mind falls back into 'FAT' mode and this is 100% ok. Now that i have learnt how to change my body, the feeling doesn't need to carry on.

Am I normal? Yes

Anxiety at the gym can be a barrier but if you keep going and take day by day, workout by workout, soon it will disappear. Don't get me wrong I still feel weird in the gym sometimes, but nowhere near as bad as I was. Having a gym buddy or a few people you can go to the gym with, makes it so much easier. Grab the girls, go to some classes or get a PT session together. The more you try the easier it will be to find your preferred style of training.

RUN to RELAX! Get them dolphins swimming. I mean endorphins ha-ha. Now, I haven't been the running kind of girl, I skipped PE at school and never liked exercise. I developed early, so big bouncy boobs and wibbly-wobbly chub meant that sports were just not my thing at the time. I always had a fear of not being able to do it or being the last one to finish or making a fool out of myself.

However, When I got to the ripe old age of 28 an interest in running took me by surprise. So, one day I asked a friend who ran a lot if I could join him on a run but warned him it may only last 30 seconds. To my surprise, I ran (slow jogged) for around 30 minutes with a few power walks. I felt amazing. So, I decided to keep running a couple of times a week and then took part in a charity 5k run. It was amazing. Since then I have completed a few more.

Whether you see yourself doing certain exercises/sports or not, give running a try, you never know how it could make you feel. Plus, its FREE!

When I started I downloaded the

app 'couch to 5k'. It's an amazing tool to get your body moving and you will be running longer and farther in no time.

Go for it! You have nothing to lose. Well, maybe a few pounds and some stress might be lost! Winner!

TOOLBOX

Gym anxiety

Go with a friend

Try a couple of classes

Book a PT session

Wear headphones and focus on yourself

Breathe deeply before entering the gym

Go at quieter times to begin with

Talk to people if you need help (People love to help)

Make new friends

Set your goals.... then smash them (FOCUS IS KEY)

REMEMBER.... everyone is there for themselves

OBSESSION

5

FOOD - I love you I love you not

Every single person whether male or female has had some type of insecurity about the way they look. It doesn't help that society is hooked to social media now. We all have one body that we were born into, different shapes, sizes, height, build, blood type, skin type, etc. Working on your health and wellbeing is one of the most effective ways to love yourself and show gratitude to your own body.

Whether you're a size 6 or 26, who has the right to judge you? The world has grown into a place of judgment, comparisons, and jealousy. Now that's unhealthy.

I'm on my journey to love myself, and albeit a cliché, if you love yourself then you will be loved. #Am I normal? #03 Love is a must read if you're wondering about loving and being loved.

It becomes unhealthy when we harm our bodies for the sake of trying to be something or look a certain way without putting in a consistent and healthy way of living,

Now, this is something I have only disclosed to two people in my life, but it only seems right to be open and talk about it when I am here giving tips about self-help and a self-love journey.

After going through my first loss to the inevitable death,

not only did I suffer from extreme anxiety, but I developed an eating disorder. Said disorder being bulimia.

Now, I was in a mental battle with myself and this is explained further in Am I Normal #No2 Mind. Typically, all body issues come from a single thought or a sequence of thoughts that have developed into beliefs and feelings.

Bulimia involves a binge eating session ending in the removal of that food by vomiting. There are different symptoms of bulimia, but this was mine. For over a year I would schedule a binge eating session in with myself and all my favourite snacks at least once a week then once I had enjoyed them all and felt a little nauseous I would take myself to the bathroom to remove it all. Sounds gross right?

Am I normal? Yes.

Eating disorders can be silent little devils and getting over shame or guilt to conquer the disorder can be challenging. But hey, we are all human and there's nothing wrong with owning up to it.

I struggled with this until recently where I have managed to control this after speaking to someone. After all, how can I preach about healthy minds and bodies if I'm not practicing it?

How do I think it started? Well, if I am honest I can't put my finger on it. I think I heard a conversation in passing one day about the disorder and somehow it wriggled its way into my subconscious. Being on a weight loss journey for over 2 years took its toll on me. Constantly trying to lose weight, limiting calories or training extra hard felt like a punishment at times. But as I learnt and am still learning, nothing worth having is easily achieved. Work hard, stay consistent and the results will be far more rewarding. The thought of bags of chocolate, bags of crisps and an 8 pack of flour wraps was heaven to me. I knew what I was doing but I just couldn't stop, it almost became my normal until I realised it needed to stop for my own health and wellbeing.

The reason I am drawing upon the relationship with food is because it's a silent issue that most people are ashamed to talk about. I keep repeating this, but society has a standard and an expectation which is completely unrealistic. There are many great public figures out there trying to make a difference and highlighting issues so that the world doesn't feel alone with their issues, but why are these issues so hard to talk about?

I just want to make it clear that it's OK if you have a toxic relationship with food, because Again, you have the power to change it. You are no different to anyone else, whether you have bulimia, anorexia, binge eating disorder etc. What does society expect when every shop you walk in has isles of discounted goodies and huge bags of chocolate for £1? The temptation is inevitable. When was the last time you saw a fruit advert or a barrel full of apples discounted on your Saturday shop?

The most important thing is that you recognise the effects on your mind and your body. Once you have accepted this then there are so many ways you can get yourself back to a healthy place with food.

TOOL BOX

Counselling and spiritual healing could be the best thing you ever do when it comes to understanding yourself and your body. For me reaching out to a spiritual healer was one of the hardest yet probably the most sensible things I have done. Therapy was a blessing. Being open to a stranger was a weird concept, but having no judgement, a safe place to cry and let out my emotions was amazing.

No one knew about my toxic relationship with food, I had kept it a secret. So, if you know me personally, this may be hard to read.
Ultimately, we all have secrets in one way or another, and this kind of secret came from a place of shame.

You will read about my spiritual journey in the next chapter, but Please read my email below which I sent to a local counselling service first. Before I go into my journey with a spiritual healer/counsellor I wanted to cover all options that I had and unfortunately a counselling service was not for me. But everyone is different. People respond to therapies in different ways so the best thing to do is try.

Once I had emailed the counselling service I knew the next step was a phone call, and because I had already outlined my problem I was prepared to answer questions and open more. In a time of need, it's hard to explain how you are feeling. But honestly, these people who are there to help and will not judge you.

'It has been recommended that i contact this service. I am struggling mentally now and i don't feel like i can make any decisions or control my emotions at all. I have been having issues with my relationship with food, but it has escalated to a point where I can't seem to stop myself.

Everything feels surreal and i have had depression for over 10 years. At times i have controlled it and focussed on becoming on a better me and living my life positively. However, my current circumstances have triggered a huge change and emotional struggle and i really am not coping at all. I felt like i couldn't call the helpline because i just keep crying and i am so scared. I am trying to not let this affect my work and i have so far been ok but i have lost my motivation to get back on the right track. i just don't know what to think or how to feel right now. Every obstacle I come across in life seems to be blown out of proportion and mainly because I have no self-confidence and my relationship with food is making things worse.

I hope you can help.'

Am I normal? Yes

I think for a lot of us, we believe that losing weight and doing a little work on ourselves will cure all our problems. But as I said at the beginning, we all go through problems that cause us to react in different ways. Life is full of ups and downs and sometimes the downs are so scary that we find a way of coping that is unhealthy for us. But it's ok, because it CAN be CHANGED. Once we recognise we need help or some guidance, then the universe will present you with that support. Don't worry.

As I mentioned, counselling services were not for me. As a spiritual person I believe I can be healed through mind work and opening my soul with spiritual doors.

However, the lady I did speak to on the phone was amazing and she asked me a set of questions that enabled her to understand where my issues were coming from. I would recommend this type of support if you are not spiritual because trained counsellors are able to dig deeper into your problems and help you to see context.

There are also lots of websites with forums and chat services that can help too. IF you are struggling with your food, just do a little

research and I promise you will find lots of useful tools.

BREATHE

6

Spiritual Journey

July 2017, a friend of mine passed away. A friend who was lively, positive and always saw the best in everyone. Now, this was my first experience of loss at the age of 28 and it completely changed my perspective on life. I always wondered if death was even real because I hadn't experienced a loss like this.

Am I normal? Yes

Well, as weeks passed by after the funeral I had a sudden feeling of emptiness, fear and it felt like I couldn't control my body. Was this an out of body experience? I couldn't get into a car without thinking I couldn't control my bowels and I felt trapped and so scared that I would just memorise every service station, calculate how long it would take me to get from A to B and how long I could sit without needing to go to the toilet.

Everywhere I went I needed to know there was a toilet, a friend or someone who could save me. Butterflies in my belly, sweat dripping from my forehead and hands so clammy I felt like I was about to face my biggest fear.

This carried on for about 2 months, I even self-diagnosed myself with IBS. I researched treatment, I cut out most foods and I avoided any social activity I could. During this time, I had an interview at the company I work for now. Unbeknown to me I must have hidden this problem well because I landed the job and my career change had begun.

Change is the keyword here. It felt like everything was changing right in front of me, but I didn't feel present.

Luckily, I overheard a conversation about mediums and spiritual healing. I was intrigued. I was given a contact to a lady who lived locally to me and the recommendations were all positive.

At this point, I would try anything to feel like me again, so I booked in and went along to see what this medium could tell about my life and what was happening to me.

To my surprise this lady was an experienced counsellor, spiritual healer and medium. As I sat in her beautiful cabin in her back garden, filled with crystals and spiritual ornaments, I felt a sense of relief. She asked me to close my eyes and imagine a bright white light. She then guided me through a meditation that would release all the fear from my body. She then went into reading about my life and what was to come, my friend who had passed was present during this reading. There were things she knew about my friends and family that there was no way she could know without being psychic, this was insane!

I explained about the feelings I was experiencing and how I just didn't feel like myself and that I could not understand what was going on.

Donna guided me through one of the toughest times of my life and I can never thank her enough for that. Every month since this visit I sat with her for an hour to meditate and talk through my fears.

I was healing.

Every time I visited Donna, she would explain how I was healing and learning to work on myself to become enlightened.

Now, you may be reading this thinking; what does this have to do with weight loss and the body and what if you're not spiritual? But what my spiritual journey is teaching me is to love all of myself, including my body.

To love the skin that I live within is my goal and it should be a goal for every human. Connecting with the body is key to understanding how thoughts will affect you mentally and physically.

For example, during this time of grief and loss of connection, I gained so much weight I also felt extremely uncomfortable in my skin. As I connected back with my body and began to quieten my mind, my love for health and fitness slowly came back to me.

It is ok to lose yourself sometimes, because I learnt so much from this experience. I was a mess during this time of my life, but the day I turned to spirituality is the day I realised I could control my mind and body through meditation and learning about myself.

This is not an instant cure, but meditation and mindfulness became a huge game changer for developing and growing within myself.

Meditation can refocus your mind and lift your spirits so high that you feel like you can conquer the world.

If you feel disconnected from your body or having trouble with your weight or your self-confidence, read the mediations in this book that you can practice anywhere at any time. You could also get a friend or a partner to read this while you close your eyes and fully immerse yourself into this mediation.

Spiritual healing can be for any issue you may be facing. You may have heard of 'Headspace' which is an app that has a set of meditations on to help to quieten the mind. During my time of extreme anxiety, I practiced the meditations that Donnas had given me, but I also used headspace, listened to sleep mediations on YouTube and read all kinds of self-help books. Learning about self-development and mind control is what kept me going.

Meditations have become a huge part of my life and something I will continue. On the toilet, in my bed, on the train and even when I'm waiting for a coffee in the local coffee shop. To control your mind is such a powerful tool, and if you start now just to be able to quieten the thoughts, the benefits will be so powerful.

JOURNEY

7

Stars and Umbrellas

As mentioned in my introduction, a concept taught to me by my mentor has had a huge impact on the way that I think about the journey of life. You're the star and the umbrellas are your journey.

The way she explained it was that every journey in your life is the opening of an umbrella.

Umbrella of Body

Let's look at my Umbrella for the Body. Although a great way to think about your journey, sometimes looking a little deeper can make things a little clearer.

My body has been a complicated journey for many years. From the age of 10 when puberty arrived, I have always been confused about changes that happened, the function of the different parts and whether I was comfortable in my body.

As I grew up, my umbrella began to open, but many times it has broken, shut down and I felt like the rain just kept pouring.

I've never felt confident in my own skin, so my journey began with what could I change?

Asking questions about how you feel within your body and the reasons why you feel that way can open the next spike of your umbrella. For example, once I realised I needed to improve on my body to help me feel more comfortable, the gym was the next part of my journey.

As I began to learn about how exercise can change my body, I learnt that food was a huge factor in my journey also. As you now already know, food has been a huge part of my life and the relationship with it has been toxic. But again, this is just another part of my journey that i am working on, so that my Umbrella can open.

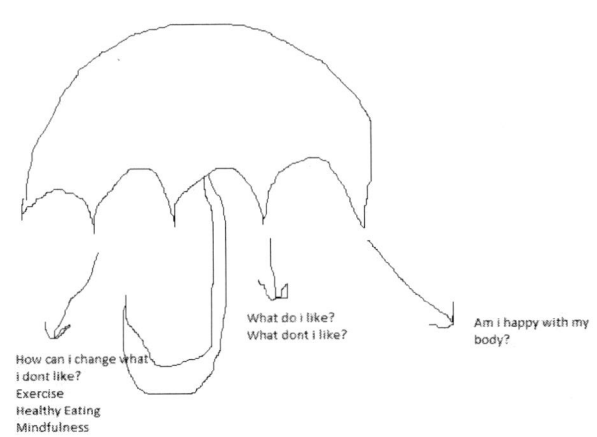

What do i like?
What dont i like?

Am i happy with my body?

How can i change what i dont like?
Exercise
Healthy Eating
Mindfulness
Detox

Asking questions relating to your journey can help you understand where you are along your journey. The goal for every individual will be different. For me, being comfortable in my skin, feeling healthy and energised is my goal.

Sometimes along the way, you may feel like giving up, you could look at this as if your umbrella was down. But, once your umbrella comes up, you are protected It's your choice to put up the umbrella, to wear a raincoat to dance naked in the rain.

8

MEDITATION

Make sure you are in a space where you will not be disturbed. You can lie down or simply sit on a chair with your arms by your side or resting on your lap. Be sure not to cross your legs or arms.

Once you are comfortable close your eyes and feel your body relax into the chair or bed. Take a deep breath in and feel love in your heart. You see a green light in your heart.

In front of you, you will see a wall. How high is this wall? If it is too high to climb over, knock it down and climb over where you will see a pathway leading down to a beach. Feel the sea breeze on your face and the heat from the sun touching your skin. Walk down to the water edge and feel the sand in between your toes. As you look up, you see a mountain with a pathway leading up. Walk up the pathway until you see a ledge on the side of the mountain. Sit down with your legs hanging over the edge and look out into the ocean. The sun is shining, you can see boats in the distance and the birds flying through the sky.

Sit for a moment and feel safe. You're safe.

Behind you, you hear water running. You stand up and walk over to a cave that has a shower inside. You undress and step into the cave. Let the water run over your head and feel a bright white light over your whole body. As the water continues to run over your head, your shoulders, your waist and down to your toes, ask the universe to make you feel comfortable and confident within your skin.

Take a deep breathe in and see the green light through your body. As you breathe out you see any negative self-talk leave your body. This could be a red light leaving your body which you turn into green light. Breathe in and take in the green light.

In front of you, there is a large grey towel. Step out of the shower and wrap yourself in the towel until your body is covered. As you look up there is a clear tube above your head. The tube begins to come down over your head, your shoulders, your waist and your toes. The tube fills with a bright white light, making you feel safe and confident. As the tube goes back up it takes any negative energy away from you.

You get dressed and begin to walk back down the mountain. You feel cleansed, refreshed and energized. You have the confidence to be and do whatever you wish. You love your body and you feel safe within your skin.

As you approach the sand, sit down and take a minute to feel the sun kiss your fresh skin. When you are ready, open your eyes.

Take a moment to come back to the space you're in. Look around you, breathe slowly and become aware again.

9

VALUES

Another tool I have learned recently is to focus on your Values. Our values inform our words, thoughts, and actions. They are important because they help us to grow and develop. When relating values to our bodies, image and self-love, it is important to understand our individual values to understand why feel and react in certain ways. Every individual is involved in making decisions every single day. Values are what we believe matter most in life. Common values are; Love, happiness, loyalty, and respect. For example, if we are not happy in our bodies and do not respect them, then how are we living by the values that we believe in?

At the grand age of 30 I am only just stepping onto this journey of finding my purpose. To figure that out, I needed to dig deeper into my values.

As children, values are passed down from our parents and elders. As we grow up, some values may stay the same, but we grow into ourselves and find values within ourselves such gratitude and tolerance. The thing is, you can't expect to discover your purpose in life if you don't know what's important to you.

My mentor Natalie, who I mentioned previously, inspired me one session to look at my values. It's not something that I had looked at before. She pulled out a deck of cards and of course I just thought we were about to play snap. Well, that was a disappointment at first.

The deck of cards had one word on each card. Natalie asked me to look through the whole deck of cards and pick 20 words that I felt a connection with. When I had picked my 20 she then asked me to pick 10 that I felt were more meaningful to me out of that 20. Once I had got to my 10 she then asked me to pick 5 that were most important to me.

This exercise was a lot harder than I thought because there were so many words that meant something to me. Once I had picked my 5 I put them in order of most important. I looked at the cards and felt a little emotional. Look at my 10 and 5 words below:

10
- EMPATHY
- HEALTH
- LOVE/AFFECTION
- SPIRITUALITY/FAITH
- TRUST
- PROSPERITY/WEALTH
- HAPPINESS
- GROWTH
- LOYALTY
- WISDOM

5
- HAPPINESS
- LOVE/AFFECTION
- TRUST
- HEALTH
- GROWTH

Out of a whole deck of cards I had managed to pick five that I instantly felt a connection with. Each word pulled on my heartstrings and that meant I truly believed these words mattered to me in life. Looking at the 5 top cards I can see my values:

Happiness is a huge value of mine, if I am not smiling and the people around me are not happy, then It affects me.

Love and affection is something I crave. I love the people around me and the feeling of being loved is something I longed for. Tough relationships and loss of self-worth over many years meant all I wanted was to be loved. It's important to me to love and to be loved.

Trust seems to be a common value after sharing my values with a few friends. If trust is not present, then anxiety strikes, and a whirlwind of insecurities enter your life. Trusting others and to be trusted is highly important in my life.

Health is something I relate to the body and mind. If both are not being taken care of then issues arise.

Finally, **growth** is extremely important to me. Expanding the mind, growing your knowledge and self-development gives your life purpose and meaning. Growth helps you to stay focused on your life goals, makes you feel alive and motivated.

When my values are compromised, or I feel I am not living up to my own values, I start to feel like I am letting myself down. However, it was great to find out what is important to me because now I have a guide. A guide that reminds me of my beliefs and takes me on a journey to discover a purpose and live a meaningful life.

On the following pages you will find a list of core values to work out what your values are.

Just like I did you could pick 20 words that mean something to you, then take that down to 10 then down to 5. This will show you what matters to you the most.

Abundance
Acceptance
Accountability
Achievement
Advancement
Adventure
Advocacy
Ambition
Appreciation
Attractiveness
Autonomy
Balance
Being the Best
Benevolence
Boldness
Brilliance
Calmness
Caring
Challenge
Charity
Cheerfulness

Cleverness
Community
Commitment
Compassion
Cooperation
Collaboration
Consistency
Contribution
Creativity
Credibility
Curiosity
Daring
Decisiveness
Dedication
Dependability
Diversity
Empathy
Encouragement
Enthusiasm
Ethics
Excellence
Expressiveness
Fairness
Family

Friendships
Flexibility
Freedom
Fun
Generosity
Grace
Growth
Happiness
Health
Honesty
Humility
Humour
Inclusiveness
Independence
Individuality
Innovation
Inspiration
Intelligence
Intuition
Joy
Kindness
Knowledge
Leadership
Learning

Love
Loyalty
Making a Difference
Mindfulness
Motivation
Optimism
Open-Mindedness
Originality
Passion
Performance
Personal Development
Proactive
Professionalism
Quality
Recognition
Risk Taking
Safety
Security
Service
Spirituality
Stability
Peace
Perfection
Playfulness

Popularity
Power
Preparedness
Proactivity
Professionalism
Punctuality
Recognition
Relationships
Reliability
Resilience
Resourcefulness
Responsibility
Responsiveness
Security
Self-Control
Selflessness
Simplicity
Stability
Success
Teamwork
Thankfulness
Thoughtfulness
Traditionalism
Trustworthiness

Understanding
Uniqueness
Usefulness
Versatility
Vision
Warmth
Wealth
Well-Being
Wisdom

1.

2.

3.

4.

5.

Keep a note of your top 5 values. Every time something annoys you, have a look at your list. You will then be able to work out why this situation has annoyed you.

UNIQUE

'She's so beautiful'

"I love your figure, you inspire me "

"Women with muscles look like men "

"Toned women are so sexy'

10

Green-eyed Monster

Sound somewhat familiar? The reason for this chapter, is to help women and men to understand that your body goals should be about becoming the best version of yourself, and not to fit into the social norm that everyone is striving to be, just because of the 'trend' or what celebrities are doing to create a body that's unobtainable to most people. A big problem we have today is that jealousy and admiration have a very thin line between them and I just want to express how this makes me feel and one way that we can control jealousy and turn it into something positive. Wanting what others possess is normal but creating a unique self and having your own inspirations and ambitions is important too.

In an ideal world, we would be complementing, supporting and enjoying life with the people around us. But we don't, and we are all guilty of being jealous at some point in our lives. Unless you were brought up in a confined space with no contact to social media, media and different groups of people, then I'm pretty sure you have been jealous or experienced jealousy in one way or another.

A little jealousy is healthy because it is an important emotion that lets you know that a relationship or situation needs attending to. This may be in the form of working on your insecurities or discussing issues with a friend, partner etc. It is healthy because it offers you a chance to connect with yourself and improve on yourself.

The list is massive but here are some examples where jealousy is formed:

Instagram - Women are photoshopping pictures to be 'ideal' for the audience

YouTube - Channels focussing on the current trend, using young girls to advertise

Reality TV programmes showing the lives of wealthy men and women

Young female music groups - wearing erm...not much

Social media as a whole! - We can see everyone's lives on one device - is it a true reflection of their lives?

This has become an issue for men also. People strive for unobtainable goals. Trends change daily, weekly, monthly and yearly. Men and women go to extremes to fit in with the social norm, rather than just accepting who they are and becoming the best version of themselves. The negative effect that social media has on people is creating insecurities and jealousy without a doubt.

In my experience and on my weight loss journey, I have developed a mindset that is based on becoming a better me.

Yes, I look at Instagram models and Fitness Videos on YouTube and yes sometimes I think 'wow, she looks good, guess that works'. But when I think outside the box, I use these images and videos to inspire me and keep me motivated. But, I do have days where I lose motivation, control and a clear mindset and that's because I'm human. I accept those days because without them I wouldn't be able to correct myself and grow.

My shape has become a trend recently. A small waist, big bum and thighs. However, when I began my journey I didn't look to see what was on trend, I simply knew I didn't feel comfortable in my own body and needed something to change because my confidence was low, and clothes did not fit me how I wished they would, As expectations grow, it seems that the man's 'ideal woman' becomes somewhat unrealistic too.

Some people are judgemental and selfish, and we don't all think the same. I've met men who have made me feel like I'm nothing and made me feel like I'm not beautiful enough, but I'm glad I have met these men because it has made me a stronger woman.

What I'm trying to say is that every one of us is unique and if you just take a few minutes a day to be grateful to be alive and realise that everything you do to improve your wellbeing, fitness, knowledge, etc, will make you a better person than you were the day before. That's all that matters.

We live in a world full of competition, jealousy, fear and so many other negative ways of living that if we just switched these habits to something positive we would be able to support and connect a lot better. After all, we all are born, we live our lives and then we die. So, make it worthwhile.

USE YOUR GREEN-EYED MONSTER AS A MOTIVATOR

As I mentioned before, a little jealousy can be healthy in all aspects of life. Regarding body confidence, other women and self-growth, it is easier to accept it when jealousy comes around.

For example, recently I kept seeing the same girl at the gym that had an amazing body and I admired her for all her hard work. I did realise I was a little bit jealous of her success, but what I did was took the emotion, admitted to myself that I had it, changed it to motivation and used my emotions to fuel my willpower. I also approached the girl at one point because I needed to use the equipment she was using and asked her how long she would be. To my surprise, she looked at me like she wanted to kill me and was extremely rude. This encounter completely changed my view of this girl, because as they say, an ugly personality can make you an ugly person. I still admire her for her hard work, but it made me realise that her arrogance and attitude towards other people was a bad trait to have. I would rather be working hard on myself and reaching for my personal goals than wasting time with the jealous emotion on someone who wouldn't even appreciate my admiration of theirs.

Another example of jealousy is when someone is constantly putting you down and judging your life. This places the jealousy on their heads. For another person to put you down and negatively target you, it means they are not happy with themselves and have their insecurities shadowing them.

So, remember that, because when I've experienced this in the past, it's hurt me, and the other person has achieved what they wanted which is for me to feel bad about myself which in turn makes them feel better about themselves. However, if it happens to me now, I use their jealousy to motivate me. Their green-eyed monster will not defeat me anymore. Again, I look at what I do have; I work on my own goals and make sure that I am creating a better version of myself every day.

So next time you feel your green-eyed monster boiling up, turn the heat down and reconnect with yourself. Step outside the box and look at why you're experiencing this emotion. Work on your goals and your happiness because that is what is important. Use your monster to motivate you and improve yourself. When browsing social media and watching TV, appreciate the hard work that your inspirations put in to look how they do. The more you appreciate them and yourself the better you will improve your self-love.

Aunt Flo

11

Mother Nature – A women's Thoughts

Believe it or not, mother nature is one of the biggest natural causes of worry, insecurities, mental breakdowns, body issues and more. I started my period at the age of 10 and as the years have gone on, my premenstrual symptoms have got worse. Abdominal cramps, Spot breakouts, fatigue, sore boobies, bloating, lower back pain, trouble sleeping, swelling and more. Once a month I must prepare for the breakdown and, warn everyone around me and wait for the storm to pass.

Aunt flo does have her positives though. A regular period tells us that we are healthy and working properly. It really is the ultimate excuse for self-care, because whilst your feeling like crap and finding every excuse not to do anything, you know it will pass and you pay more attention to your body and how you can improve your overall health.

The great news is, it lets you know you're not pregnant *sigh of relief* for some, obviously not if you are wanting to get pregnant.

Another great benefit is that it can warn you about future diseases. Women must be very observant when it comes to their bodies, whether we like it or not, checking blood colour, detecting a difference in odour and monitoring discharge.

Yes, I know for you men you're probably wondering why I am going into the uncomfortable subject of periods, but for women and men it really is important to understand the women's body. after all, women are the ones who can carry a baby for 9 months. High five ladies.

Another positive of having periods is that it helps you live longer. I have done so much research into periods because I have struggle for over 20 years now with the side effects.

When you know the benefits of aunt flo, you will be more welcoming of her. Whenever you menstruate, your body discharges iron, one of the major reasons why your period makes you young. Looking at studies based on longevity, iron loss can help reduce the risk of stroke and heart disease.

For the men reading this, it's just a quick reminder that women do experience a change in their bodies every month. SO, give her a break when its coming, when the hormones levels are high and all she wants is a bag of chocolate and a cuddle.

This brings me onto the side effects. The hormonal changes can cause mood changes. Unfortunately for many of us there isn't much we can do to prevent it, but there are ways of coping with it.

For me, I start to experience mood changes the week before I'm due on. Unexpected tears, a huge craving for chocolate and a short temper. My body swells, I feel uncomfortable in all my clothes and everything seems like such an effort.

Am I normal? Yes

Yes, I am. I have spoken to so many other women around this subject, and nearly all agree or have similar symptoms.

Sometimes the mood swings can be so bad that i almost fall into a depression every single month. I have found the key to dealing with this is letting the people around you know what's happening. It's not their fault after all. But once they know, it can make it easier to just go with the FLO.

I spent a lot of years feeling guilty after my period because I had eaten too much or snapped at my loved ones and cried and the most ridiculous things. But, these things are normal, so I choose now to go through it and after I focus on my self-care and ways to improve on myself.

As I mentioned at the beginning of this book, our bodies are our house. IF we looked after them and get them in order, then maybe we will live a happier life whilst we are in them.

As for anything that effects our mood and or makes us feel negatively about our bodies, choose to look at the positives instead. What wonderful bodies we have, how amazing are the things that they can do Aunt Flo, you are welcome.

BEAUTY

12

Wake up and Makeup

Life is not a fashion show, but you should feel good and let's face it, when you're making changes to be a better you, you do what makes you happy and comfortable.

So, this section is about wearing makeup. Why? Because I've had a few people ask me as a makeup artist, do I wear makeup at the gym? the answer is yes. If I was to wear no makeup, my face would look like a bit of paper next to my body (I love a bit of fake tan when I haven't been on holiday).

I am human after all and I do what makes me happy. Don't get me wrong, that has taken me approximately 28 years of my life to do, but I now do what makes me happy, confident and comfortable.

I don't wear an awful lot of makeup at the gym but it's enough just to give me a fresh and natural look whilst working out. Now, because I mainly do weights in my workouts I don't sweat an awful lot, this means I don't walk out looking like a drowned rat. However, when i do cardio, i do. But I still wear the same makeup every time i go. I find that the mineral-based complexion products stay on my skin and do not go patchy once i have been sweating. A good waterproof mascara will not run down your face and your eyebrows but be prepared for a few smudges here and there.

If you're cleansing, toning and moisturising after your workout then you should not experience any issues. When i first started training, i did have sweat rashes, now that's not from makeup but my body and skin adjusting to temperature changes and excess sweat. Exfoliating twice a week removes excess dead skin cells and lets my skin renew itself. A good skin routine is always advised. My skin care routine is very simple, i use Liz Earle cleanse and polish to cleanse and I use Vitamin E oil as my moisturiser day and night. I exfoliate with the Liz Earle exfoliator twice a week and use the clay mask twice a week also.

Wearing makeup to the gym is a personal preference. I wear makeup to the gym because that's what i want to do. Keep it simple, natural and make sure your skincare routine is on point. But, if you choose not to wear makeup then again keep on top of your skincare routine because the sweat will affect your skin regardless.

My message to you here is that if you want to wear makeup to the gym then do it. It's no one business to judge you. Like I said previously if you find things that make you feel comfortable then do it. If wearing a onesie in the gym with swimming goggles on makes you feel comfortable then do it!

13

YOU ARE NORMAL

In this little book of comfort, I have opened up to you about some of my own experiences in life. I hope you take some comfort in knowing that you are not alone with whatever obstacle you may be up against right now or something you have experienced before.

You may not even relate to my experiences at all, but what I do hope you can take from this is a little comfort in any self-doubts you may have.

Every human is born into a body that is unique and is theirs to look after forever. There's no such thing as normal, honestly! Some have big boobs, some have 3 nipples, some have dark skin, some have freckly skin, some have big bums, some have small heads and the list goes on and on.

Who even defined normal? Society did. Well what if working on yourself, finding love within your heart and being grateful for every inch of your body because it's your house and you deserve to feel amazing was normal?

After every obstacle I come across in my life that changes the way I feel about my body, I truly believe it has helped me to understand myself more and mould me into the woman I am today. I still have insecurities and a love hate relationship with food, but I know soon that will disappear the more I work on my inner strength and understanding.

Every day is a new day to show gratitude and fall in love with this unique body I have been blessed with.

Am I normal?

Yes

14

Meditation

Please note, this meditation has questions that help you to imagine and visualise. Questions that prompt a picture in your mind can expand your imagination.

Make sure you are in a space where you will not be disturbed. You can lie down or simply sit on a chair with your arms by your side or resting on your lap. Be sure not to cross your legs or arms.

Once you are comfortable close your eyes and feel your body relax into the chair or bed. Take a deep breath in and feel love in your heart. You see a green light in your heart.

In front of you there is a wall. If the wall is high, I want you to lower it. Step over the wall and you walk into a garden. In the garden there are animals, there are tree, birds and you can smell the fresh perfume of the flowers surrounding the garden. It's relaxing.

You see a pathway. You walk along the pathway, and alongside you are trees and flowers and you feel at peace.

In front of you, you see your dream house. Think about how big it is, what surrounds the house and who might be at the house.

As you approach your dream house, you stand in front of it for a moment to appreciate the calmness and serenity that this building gives you.

What does the front door look like? What colour is it?

You open the door and you enter your dream house. In front of you, you see the stairs to the bedrooms, you walk up the stairs. How many rooms are there?

You walk into the first room that you see. What colour is it?

If you see a dark colour, turn the colour to white. What do you see in this room? Is this your bedroom? Or the kids bedroom? Or maybe even a guest bedroom?

How do you feel in this room?

You now exit this room and enter another room. What colour is this room? If it is a dark colour, turn it to white or green. How do you feel in this room?

As you enter each room, think about how you feel. Do you feel happy, safe, overwhelmed or maybe even at peace?

Try to feel positive in all these rooms.

You walk back down the stairs. What rooms do you see? Is anyone there?

Find a chair and sit down here for a moment. You feel at peace. You feel relaxed. You feel a warm energy flowing around your body.

As you stand up from the chair, you walk towards the front door and walk out into the sunshine. Close the door and make your way back along the pathway. Birds are singing, trees are swaying, the flowers are bright, and you feel happy and safe.

When you are ready, come back to your chair and open your eyes.

This mediation is great for feeling safe. If you suffer from anxiety or worry a lot, use this meditation to go to a safe place. You can repeat this mediation and change your house or the surroundings as many times as you like until you are clear on what it looks like. This is one of the first meditations I practiced with Donna and I still do this now when I feel uneasy or nervous.

It's also amazing if someone can read this to you as they can ask more questions to trigger your imagination.

When I do this mediation now it's almost like visiting my future house, where I have a pool, a huge kitchen, a beautiful bedroom where I chill on the balcony with my boyfriend and watch the sunrise and sunset.

Hey, Visualisation is a powerful tool, maybe I will live in this house one day.

In my next book 'Am I Normal #2 Mind' you will find more meditations.

I hope this has given you a little comfort or maybe even inspired you.

Take care humans.

Vikki x

Author: Vikki Kinge

Illustrations: Vikki Kinge
Proof Editor: Naomi Matzen
Published: 2019

Printed in Poland
by Amazon Fulfillment
Poland Sp. z o.o., Wrocław